WOODRIDGE PUBLIC LIBRARY
W9-CKL-761

First Facts™

Holidays and Culture

Martin Luther King Jr. Day

Honoring a Civil Rights Hero

by Amanda Doering

Consultant:
Sandra Adell, Professor of Literature
Department of Afro-American Studies
University of Wisconsin, Madison

Capstone
press
Mankato, Minnesota

First Facts is published by Capstone Press,
151 Good Counsel Drive, P.O. Box 669, Mankato, Minnesota 56002.
www.capstonepress.com

Library of Congress Cataloging-in-Publication Data
Doering, Amanda.
Martin Luther King Jr. Day: honoring a Civil Rights hero/ by Amanda Doering.
p. cm.—(First facts. Holidays and culture)
Summary: "A brief description of the U.S. holiday Martin Luther King Jr. Day, including how it started, and ways people celebrate this cultural holiday"—Provided by publisher.
Includes bibliographical references and index.
ISBN-13: 978-0-7368-5391-0 (hardcover)
ISBN-10: 0-7368-5391-X (hardcover)
1. Martin Luther King, Jr., Day—Juvenile literature. 2. King, Martin Luther, Jr., 1929–1968 Juvenile literature. I. Title. II. Series.
E185.97.K5D655 2006
323'.092—dc22 2005020072

Editorial Credits

Christine Peterson, editor; Juliette Peters, designer; Wanda Winch, photo researcher; Scott Thoms, photo editor

Photo Credits

Capstone Press/Karon Dubke, 21
Corbis/Bettmann, 8, 12, 13, 14–15
Getty Images/Time Life Pictures/Diana Walker, 16; Francis Miller, 10–11; Howard Sochurek, 1; Stan Wayman, 9
Greater Philadelphia Martin Luther King Day of Service/Todd W. Bernstein, 20
PhotoEdit Inc./David Young-Wolff, cover, 4–5; Jeff Greenberg, 18–19
SuperStock/SuperStock Inc., 7

1 2 3 4 5 6 11 10 09 08 07 06

Table of Contents

Celebrating Martin Luther King Jr. Day

People of all **races** sing as they walk in a peace parade. Speakers tell of a man who worked to gain equal **rights** for all people. These people are celebrating Martin Luther King Jr. Day. On the third Monday in January, people honor the life and dreams of Dr. Martin Luther King Jr.

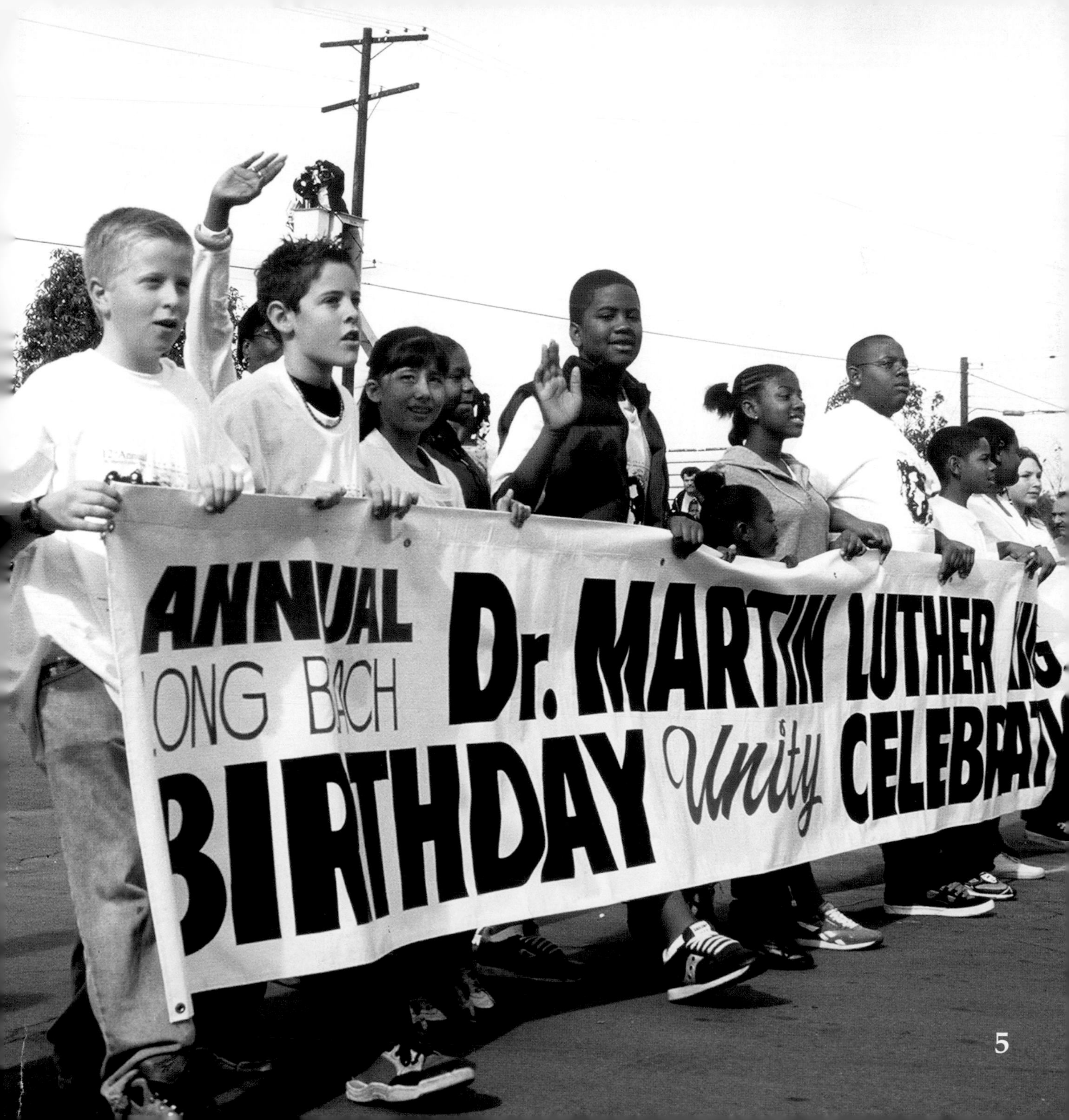
ANNUAL
Dr. MARTIN LUTHER
BIRTHDAY
Unity

What Is Martin Luther King Jr. Day?

Martin Luther King Jr. Day is a U.S. holiday. King was a minister in Atlanta, Georgia. In the 1960s, King was a leader of the **civil rights movement**.

King worked to earn equal rights for black people. Equality and freedom are important parts of the U.S. **culture**. Because of King's work, people of all races have the same freedoms.

Fact!

King is the first American since George Washington to have a national holiday in his honor.

Segregation

In the 1960s, blacks and whites were **segregated**. Black children and white children went to different schools. They couldn't eat at the same restaurants.

Blacks were forced to follow unfair laws called **Jim Crow laws**. In some southern states, blacks could not vote. They had to sit in the back of city buses.

NEWS HQ

The Civil Rights Movement

King held peace marches to change unfair laws. In 1963, King told of his dream for equality. At least 250,000 marchers listened to his "I Have a Dream" speech.

King spoke out against violence. He believed laws could be changed in a peaceful way.

Fact!

A reading of King's "I Have a Dream" speech is part of most Martin Luther King Jr. Day celebrations.

Change Comes Slowly

King's peaceful marches worked. In 1964, segregation was made illegal. Whites and blacks could go to the same schools. Blacks were allowed to vote.

Many whites still opposed equal rights for blacks. Violence against blacks was common. People threatened to kill King.

He Gave His Life

On April 4, 1968, King was killed by James Earl Ray. Ray was against equal rights. People around the world were saddened by King's death.

Four days later, U.S. Representative John Conyers asked that King's birthday be made a holiday. The government turned down Conyers' idea.

At least 100,000 people attended King's funeral in Atlanta.

Making a Holiday

Conyers kept working to honor King with a holiday. He gathered the names of 6 million people who also wanted a holiday for King. In 1983, President Ronald Reagan signed a law to make King's birthday a national holiday. The first Martin Luther King Jr. Day was celebrated in 1986.

Fact!

Although Martin Luther King Jr. was born January 17, 1929, the holiday is celebrated the third Monday in January.

Remembering King

People of all races celebrate Martin Luther King Jr. Day. Some people go to church. Others walk in peace marches. Some listen to recordings of King's speeches. People celebrate the holiday to remember King's dream of equal rights for everyone.

Most government offices and schools are closed on Martin Luther King Jr. Day.

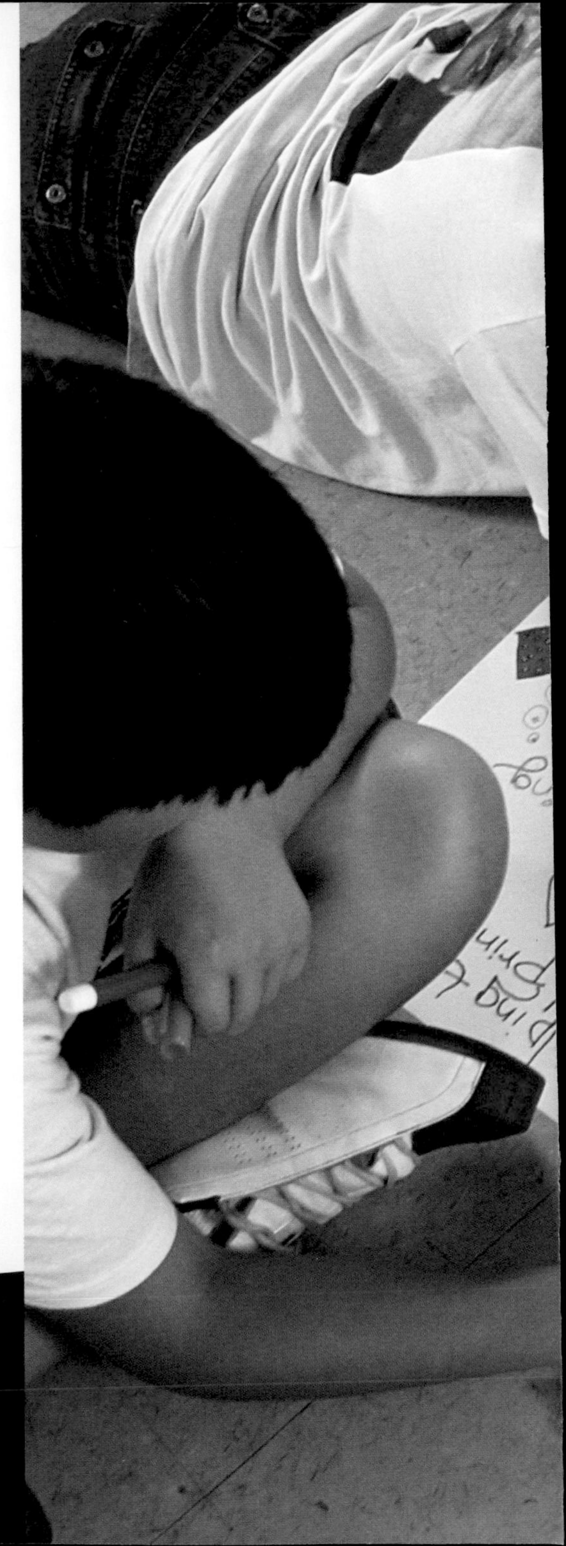

Baby
your school
Environment
Animal Rescue

Amazing Holiday Story!

In Philadelphia, Martin Luther King Jr. Day is a time to help others. At least 45,000 people join in the Martin Luther King Jr. Day of Service. People of all races join hands in peace marches. They read books. People share ideas to make their community safe. Volunteers bring food to those in need. By helping others, people in Philadelphia continue King's work for peace and equal rights.

Hands On: Chain of Hands

Dr. Martin Luther King Jr. believed in equal rights for all people. Have an adult help you make this chain of hands to show how people of all races can join together.

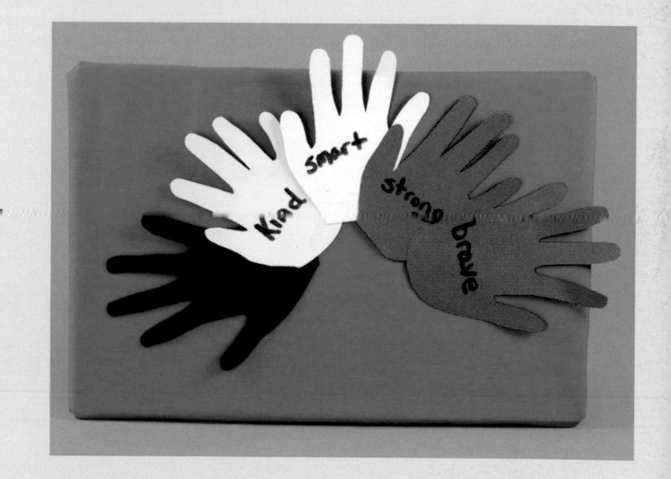

What You Need

pencil
black, yellow, white, red, and brown construction paper
scissors
a group of friends
tape

What You Do

1. Trace your hand on a piece of construction paper.
2. Use a scissors to cut out your paper hand.
3. Have your friends trace their hands on construction paper. Use a scissors to cut out the hands.
4. On each hand, write a word that describes King, such as kind, smart, caring, brave, strong, or peaceful.
5. Tape the hands together to form a long chain. Display the chain in your classroom or at home.

Glossary

civil rights movement (SIV-il RITES MOOV-muhnt)—the work of thousands of people in the mid-1900s to gain equal rights for all people

culture (KUHL-chur)—a people's way of life, ideas, art, customs, and traditions

Jim Crow laws (JIM KROH LAWZ)—laws saying that blacks and whites should live separately

race (RAYSS)—a group of people with the same background

rights (RITES)—what the law says people can have or do

segregation (seg-ruh-GAY-shuhn)—the act of keeping people or groups apart

Read More

Graves, Kerry A. *I Have a Dream: The Story Behind Martin Luther King Jr.'s Most Famous Speech.* America in Words and Song. Philadelphia: Chelsea Clubhouse, 2004.

Kaplan, Leslie C. *Martin Luther King Jr. Day.* The Library of Holidays. New York: PowerKids Press, 2004.

Internet Sites

FactHound offers a safe, fun way to find Internet sites related to this book. All of the sites on FactHound have been researched by our staff.

Here's how:

1. Visit *www.facthound.com*
2. Type in this special code **073685391X** for age-appropriate sites. Or enter a search word related to this book for a more general search.
3. Click on the **Fetch It** button.

FactHound will fetch the best sites for you!

Index